369
Laws of Attraction
Guided Workbook

chartwell
books

Inspiring | Educating | Creating | Entertaining

Brimming with creative inspiration, how-to projects, and useful information to enrich your everyday life, quarto.com is a favorite destination for those pursuing their interests and passions.

Published in 2023 by Chartwell Books,
an imprint of The Quarto Group
142 West 36th Street, 4th Floor
New York, NY 10018 USA
T (212) 779-4972 F (212) 779-6058
www.Quarto.com

10 9 8 7 6 5 4 3 2 1

Chartwell titles are also available at discount for retail, wholesale, promotional, and bulk purchase. For details, contact the Special Sales Manager by email at specialsales@quarto.com or by mail at The Quarto Group, Attn: Special Sales Manager, 100 Cummings Center Suite 265D, Beverly, MA 01915, USA.

ISBN: 978-0-7858-4210-1

Publisher: Wendy Friedman
Senior Managing Editor: Meredith Mennitt
Senior Design Manager: Michael Caputo
Editor: Joanne O'Sullivan
Designer: Sue Boylan

Printed in China

This book provides general information. It should not be relied upon as recommending or promoting any specific diagnosis or method of treatment for a particular condition. It is not intended as a substitute for medical advice or for direct diagnosis and treatment of a medical or psychological condition by a qualified physician or therapist. Readers who have questions about a particular condition, possible treatments for that condition, or possible reactions from the condition or its treatment should consult a physician, therapist, or other qualified healthcare professional.

Discover your inner
power to make
your life anything you
can imagine

369
Laws of
Attraction

Guided Workbook

INSPIRED BY THE MATHEMATICAL THEORIES OF NIKOLA TESLA

chartwell
books

Manifesting Your Dreams the 369 Way

Can you change your future by focusing positive energy in the direction of your dreams? Yes, you can, and this book will help you start.

The law of attraction is not a new concept. It's been practiced in many cultures around the world for centuries. The idea is simple. Positive thoughts bring about positive results, and the opposite is also true. Manifesting takes positive thinking one step further. Beyond just thinking positively, manifesting adds the power of words and ritual to your thoughts.

The 369 method of manifesting is a new lens on this ancient practice. To follow this method, you write your intentions three times in the morning, six times in the afternoon, and nine times at night. To be successful, all you need is some thoughtful intentions, something to write with and, of course, this workbook.

The 369 Method

The famed inventor Nikola Tesla believed that the numbers 3, 6, and 9 are key to tapping into the energy of the universe. That's why the 369 method of manifesting is thought to be so powerful. Ready to tap into that power?

The 369 method is simple: using the 369 Method templates, write down your manifestation statements three times as soon as you wake up. In the afternoon, write your manifestation statements six times. Finally, in the evening before bed, write them nine times. The repeated consistency, frequency, and intention will start to take root within you, and, over time, you will begin to embody and attract your manifestation.

You don't have to do this exercise every day. But you might want to try it three days a week or at least on a regular basis.

Why Use a Guided Workbook?

Intention needs attention. By writing down your intentions and affirmations, you are bringing your energy to them. That's essential to your success. By keeping track of them and committing to them, you're on your path to reaching them. You will activate the energy that's critical to achieving your dreams.

The templates and prompts provided in this workbook will give you the structure and daily motivation you need on your journey. Bit by bit, each day, you will channel your energy into your dreams. You'll start to notice them getting closer. You will see them on the horizon.

How to Use This Book

Change doesn't happen overnight. We provide 100 templates for your manifestation journey. By committing to manifesting 100 times, you will experience the benefits of continuous growth and change. You can start your manifestation at any time. Why not start tomorrow? This workbook is designed to be customized to fit with a schedule that will guarantee your success.

Along with your manifestation statements, we'll remind you of the steps you need to take to reach your dreams and offer reflections to help you get there.

Guidelines for Creating Intention-Setting Statements and Affirmations

At its core, manifestation is about identifying what you want to bring into your life and creating that outcome. It is deeply personal. Manifesting involves two activities that change your mindset. One is creating intentions statements for your actions. "I intend to eat healthy today." Creating a specific intention-setting statement helps us focus our subconscious and visualize that reality.

A positive affirmation is a statement of belief or attitude you want to internalize and manifest. Affirmations change your generalized attitudes about yourself and your life. They are usually not as specific as the intention-setting statements you'll write every day on your templates.

An effective intention or affirmation is written in the present tense and centers on you. That means you must use "I am" rather than "I will." For our intention-setting statements and affirmations to work, we must truly believe them when we are saying them.

Why does manifestation work? Your positive belief will imbue your thoughts with positive energy. That energy has transformative power.

On the following pages there are examples of helpful positive affirmations that relate to different areas of your life. Use them as a guide for creating your own affirmations.

Affirming Your
Self-Worth

I am enough.

I define my own success.

I am proud of myself.

I achieve whatever I desire.

I am whole.

I have everything inside me I need for success.

I am capable.

I am abundant.

Use this space to commit to affirmations or intention-setting statements that will help you to achieve self-esteem.

I achieve my dreams.

Affirming Your
Health &
Body Image

I am in control of my body.

I am grateful for my body.

I am attractive.

I achieve whatever I desire.

My body is an extension of my beautiful self.

Looking and feeling good comes naturally to me.

I am at peace with how I look.

My body is coursing with healthy energy.

Use this space to commit to affirmations or intention-setting statements that will help you to achieve your health and body dreams.

My body helps me achieve my dreams.

I am in control of how I feel about my body.

My body is perfect the way it is.

Affirming Your
Career Goals

I'm becoming more skilled every day.

I have something valuable to offer the world.

I wake up every day inspired by my work.

I always achieve my work goals.

I am driven towards success.

Every day I am getting closer and closer to my dream job.

I let go of my work-related stress.

I know I will find my dream job.

Use this space to write your own affirmations or intention-setting statements for your career and work life.

I'm a magnet for great job opportunities.

I trust the process.

Attracting
Wealth

I can handle financial success.

I have a wealth mindset.

I will have all that comes with financial freedom.

I have the power to attract money.

Money will help me to help others.

I have all the money I need.

Money gives me the opportunities I desire.

I make good decisions about money.

I deserve financial security.

Use this space to commit to affirmations or intention-setting statements that will help you to achieve your financial dreams.

I will be financially free.

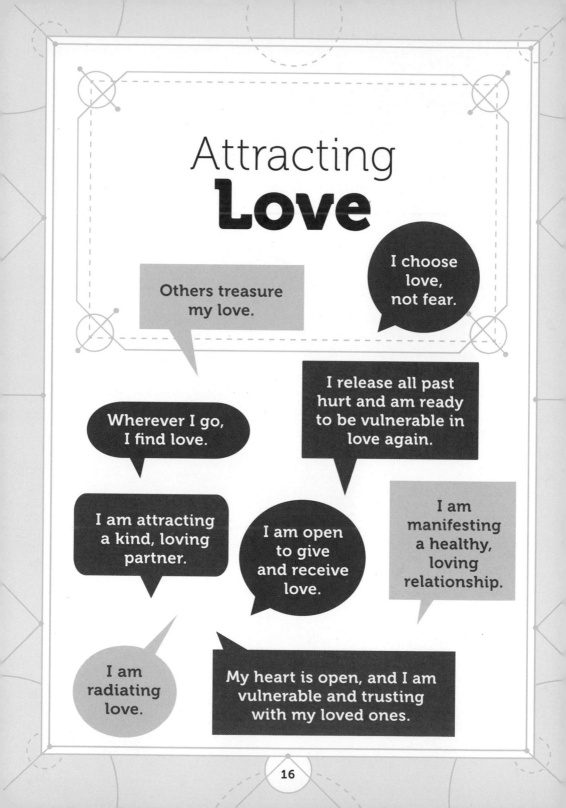

Attracting Love

Others treasure my love.

I choose love, not fear.

Wherever I go, I find love.

I release all past hurt and am ready to be vulnerable in love again.

I am attracting a kind, loving partner.

I am open to give and receive love.

I am manifesting a healthy, loving relationship.

I am radiating love.

My heart is open, and I am vulnerable and trusting with my loved ones.

The love I am seeking is seeking me.

I am ready to meet my soulmate.

I am worthy of love.

I will be happy in my next relationship

Use this space for writing your own love affirmations or intention-setting statements.

I am choosing and not waiting to be chosen.

1

Journaling

Once you
make a
decision,
the universe
conspires
to make it
happen.

—Ralph Waldo Emerson

Keeping a Journal

Journaling is one of the main ways through which you can manifest your intentions. It goes beyond the 369 method. Journaling involves more detail than your three daily affirmation sessions. Use these prompts to begin journaling at this more detailed level.

- What will it feel like when you achieve your dreams? Imagine that feeling and record it here so you can begin to manifest that energy now.

- Imagine a scene when you have just achieved that which you hope to manifest.

Write that scene with as much detail as you can. What are you wearing? Who is with you? What can you see and hear around you?

Write about how you are able to see this as a sign that you have been transformed.

Making Way

In order for your manifestation to arrive, you must clear the way and make space for it in your life. Just as we declutter our homes to make way for something new, you have to declutter your mind from old thoughts and patterns that are limiting.

Use this space to write down thoughts that are preventing you from reaching your dreams. Once you've identified them very specifically, write down very detailed plans for getting rid of these limiting beliefs. Remember, you must internalize these plans and act upon them!

DAILY 369 METHOD

MORNING: Write your manifestation statement
3 times when you first wake up.

1. _____
2. _____
3. _____

MIDDAY: (Daily Gratitude) Write 6 things
you are grateful to have in your life.

1. _____
2. _____
3. _____
4. _____
5. _____
6. _____

NIGHT: Before you go to bed, write out
your manifestation statement 9 times.

1. _____
2. _____
3. _____
4. _____
5. _____
6. _____
7. _____
8. _____
9. _____

DAILY 369 METHOD

MORNING: Write your manifestation statement
3 times when you first wake up.

1. _____
2. _____
3. _____

MIDDAY: (Daily Gratitude) Write 6 things
you are grateful to have in your life.

1. _____
2. _____
3. _____
4. _____
5. _____
6. _____

NIGHT: Before you go to bed, write out
your manifestation statement 9 times.

1. _____
2. _____
3. _____
4. _____
5. _____
6. _____
7. _____
8. _____
9. _____

DAILY 369 METHOD

MORNING: Write your manifestation statement
3 times when you first wake up.

1. _____
2. _____
3. _____

MIDDAY: (Daily Gratitude) Write 6 things
you are grateful to have in your life.

1. _____
2. _____
3. _____
4. _____
5. _____
6. _____

NIGHT: Before you go to bed, write out
your manifestation statement 9 times.

1. _____
2. _____
3. _____
4. _____
5. _____
6. _____
7. _____
8. _____
9. _____

DAILY 369 METHOD

MORNING: Write your manifestation statement
3 times when you first wake up.

1. _____
2. _____
3. _____

MIDDAY: (Daily Gratitude) Write 6 things
you are grateful to have in your life.

1. _____
2. _____
3. _____
4. _____
5. _____
6. _____

NIGHT: Before you go to bed, write out
your manifestation statement 9 times.

1. _____
2. _____
3. _____
4. _____
5. _____
6. _____
7. _____
8. _____
9. _____

DAILY 369 METHOD

MORNING: Write your manifestation statement
3 times when you first wake up.

1. _____
2. _____
3. _____

MIDDAY: (Daily Gratitude) Write 6 things
you are grateful to have in your life.

1. _____
2. _____
3. _____
4. _____
5. _____
6. _____

NIGHT: Before you go to bed, write out
your manifestation statement 9 times.

1. _____
2. _____
3. _____
4. _____
5. _____
6. _____
7. _____
8. _____
9. _____

DAILY 369 METHOD

MORNING: Write your manifestation statement
3 times when you first wake up.

1. _____
2. _____
3. _____

MIDDAY: (Daily Gratitude) Write 6 things
you are grateful to have in your life.

1. _____
2. _____
3. _____
4. _____
5. _____
6. _____

NIGHT: Before you go to bed, write out
your manifestation statement 9 times.

1. _____
2. _____
3. _____
4. _____
5. _____
6. _____
7. _____
8. _____
9. _____

DAILY 369 METHOD

MORNING: Write your manifestation statement
3 times when you first wake up.

1. _____
2. _____
3. _____

MIDDAY: (Daily Gratitude) Write 6 things
you are grateful to have in your life.

1. _____
2. _____
3. _____
4. _____
5. _____
6. _____

NIGHT: Before you go to bed, write out
your manifestation statement 9 times.

1. _____
2. _____
3. _____
4. _____
5. _____
6. _____
7. _____
8. _____
9. _____

DAILY 369 METHOD

MORNING: Write your manifestation statement
3 times when you first wake up.

1. _____
2. _____
3. _____

MIDDAY: (Daily Gratitude) Write 6 things
you are grateful to have in your life.

1. _____
2. _____
3. _____
4. _____
5. _____
6. _____

NIGHT: Before you go to bed, write out
your manifestation statement 9 times.

1. _____
2. _____
3. _____
4. _____
5. _____
6. _____
7. _____
8. _____
9. _____

2

Self-Belief

Self-realization
is the process
of manifesting
your highest
possibility of
potential in this
lifetime.

—Paramahansa Yogananda

Practicing Self-Belief

To manifest your dreams, you'll have to rely heavily on belief in yourself. That can be easier said than done. Sometimes it is easier to help others be confident and to believe in the potential of others than in ourselves.

Use this space to write some of the encouraging words you have used with your friends, such as "I believe in you," "You've got this," and "I know you are going to be successful." When you are finished, say these things aloud to yourself. Practice sitting with these thoughts until you can truly believe them.

DAILY 369 METHOD

MORNING: Write your manifestation statement
3 times when you first wake up.

1. _____
2. _____
3. _____

MIDDAY: (Daily Gratitude) Write 6 things
you are grateful to have in your life.

1. _____
2. _____
3. _____
4. _____
5. _____
6. _____

NIGHT: Before you go to bed, write out
your manifestation statement 9 times.

1. _____
2. _____
3. _____
4. _____
5. _____
6. _____
7. _____
8. _____
9. _____

DAILY 369 METHOD

MORNING: Write your manifestation statement
3 times when you first wake up.

1. _____
2. _____
3. _____

MIDDAY: (Daily Gratitude) Write 6 things
you are grateful to have in your life.

1. _____
2. _____
3. _____
4. _____
5. _____
6. _____

NIGHT: Before you go to bed, write out
your manifestation statement 9 times.

1. _____
2. _____
3. _____
4. _____
5. _____
6. _____
7. _____
8. _____
9. _____

DAILY **369** METHOD

MORNING: Write your manifestation statement
3 times when you first wake up.

1. _____
2. _____
3. _____

MIDDAY: (Daily Gratitude) Write 6 things
you are grateful to have in your life.

1. _____
2. _____
3. _____
4. _____
5. _____
6. _____

NIGHT: Before you go to bed, write out
your manifestation statement 9 times.

1. _____
2. _____
3. _____
4. _____
5. _____
6. _____
7. _____
8. _____
9. _____

DAILY 369 METHOD

MORNING: Write your manifestation statement
3 times when you first wake up.

1. _____
2. _____
3. _____

MIDDAY: (Daily Gratitude) Write 6 things
you are grateful to have in your life.

1. _____
2. _____
3. _____
4. _____
5. _____
6. _____

NIGHT: Before you go to bed, write out
your manifestation statement 9 times.

1. _____
2. _____
3. _____
4. _____
5. _____
6. _____
7. _____
8. _____
9. _____

DAILY 369 METHOD

MORNING: Write your manifestation statement
3 times when you first wake up.

1.
2.
3.

MIDDAY: (Daily Gratitude) Write 6 things
you are grateful to have in your life.

1.
2.
3.
4.
5.
6.

NIGHT: Before you go to bed, write out
your manifestation statement 9 times.

1.
2.
3.
4.
5.
6.
7.
8.
9.

DAILY 369 METHOD

MORNING: Write your manifestation statement
3 times when you first wake up.

1.
2.
3.

MIDDAY: (Daily Gratitude) Write 6 things
you are grateful to have in your life.

1.
2.
3.
4.
5.
6.

NIGHT: Before you go to bed, write out
your manifestation statement 9 times.

1.
2.
3.
4.
5.
6.
7.
8.
9.

DAILY 369 METHOD

MORNING: Write your manifestation statement
3 times when you first wake up.

1. _____
2. _____
3. _____

MIDDAY: (Daily Gratitude) Write 6 things
you are grateful to have in your life.

1. _____
2. _____
3. _____
4. _____
5. _____
6. _____

NIGHT: Before you go to bed, write out
your manifestation statement 9 times.

1. _____
2. _____
3. _____
4. _____
5. _____
6. _____
7. _____
8. _____
9. _____

DAILY 369 METHOD

MORNING: Write your manifestation statement
3 times when you first wake up.

1. _____
2. _____
3. _____

MIDDAY: (Daily Gratitude) Write 6 things
you are grateful to have in your life.

1. _____
2. _____
3. _____
4. _____
5. _____
6. _____

NIGHT: Before you go to bed, write out
your manifestation statement 9 times.

1. _____
2. _____
3. _____
4. _____
5. _____
6. _____
7. _____
8. _____
9. _____

3

Visualization

What you seek is seeking you.

—Rumi

Daydreaming with Purpose

Visualization is an important part of manifestation. It requires that you create a very compelling—a very real—image in your mind that will activate your energy and attract your dreams to you. Visualization is more than daydreaming. Some describe visualization as daydreaming with a purpose. Some call it a mental rehearsal for your future self. It's not something that necessarily comes naturally—you've got to practice. When you think about it, you have visualized before. Have you had to follow a trail, looking ahead of you to anticipate where you're going? That's similar to the process you'll use to visualize your success.

Use this space to visualize a future you. Use sensory details to capture your surroundings—sights, sounds, taste, touch, light and temperature. Now focus on yourself. Write down the emotions you're experiencing as you embody the achievement of your goals.

Embodying Your Success

Visualization can help shift your energy toward your desire. The important thing about visualizing is to try to do it very deeply. You have to 'program' your mind, body, and spirit to create the energy needed for the new reality you are trying to usher in. Use this space to practice that skill.

Imagine the obstacles you described on pages 22-23. Now imagine they are turning into liquid, then vapor, and escaping out of you. Describe what it feels like to be rid of these limiting factors.

Get in a comfortable sitting position. Do a 'body scan,' starting with your feet then moving to your ankles and up your body. As you become aware of the sensation you feel in each part of your body, imagine how it will feel when you are completely humming with the energy of success. Describe that feeling here.

Vision Boards

A vision board can help you to align energy behind your dreams. It can be an actual bulletin board, or you can use this workbook to serve as your board. On a vision board, you'll place visual reminders of what you want to manifest. Maybe it's pictures of your new house, a new love, or a new you. You can draw them or cut them out of magazines and tape them in. You can cut out or stamp words or do watercolors: whatever inspires you.

The only rule is to leave out that which you choose to leave behind. For example, if you envision a life without smoking, don't put a cigarette on your board, even with an x through it.

DAILY 369 METHOD

MORNING: Write your manifestation statement
3 times when you first wake up.

1. _____
2. _____
3. _____

MIDDAY: (Daily Gratitude) Write 6 things
you are grateful to have in your life.

1. _____
2. _____
3. _____
4. _____
5. _____
6. _____

NIGHT: Before you go to bed, write out
your manifestation statement 9 times.

1. _____
2. _____
3. _____
4. _____
5. _____
6. _____
7. _____
8. _____
9. _____

DAILY 369 METHOD

MORNING: Write your manifestation statement
3 times when you first wake up.

1. _____
2. _____
3. _____

MIDDAY: (Daily Gratitude) Write 6 things
you are grateful to have in your life.

1. _____
2. _____
3. _____
4. _____
5. _____
6. _____

NIGHT: Before you go to bed, write out
your manifestation statement 9 times.

1. _____
2. _____
3. _____
4. _____
5. _____
6. _____
7. _____
8. _____
9. _____

DAILY 369 METHOD

MORNING: Write your manifestation statement
3 times when you first wake up.

1. _____
2. _____
3. _____

MIDDAY: (Daily Gratitude) Write 6 things
you are grateful to have in your life.

1. _____
2. _____
3. _____
4. _____
5. _____
6. _____

NIGHT: Before you go to bed, write out
your manifestation statement 9 times.

1. _____
2. _____
3. _____
4. _____
5. _____
6. _____
7. _____
8. _____
9. _____

DAILY 369 METHOD

MORNING: Write your manifestation statement
3 times when you first wake up.

1. _____
2. _____
3. _____

MIDDAY: (Daily Gratitude) Write 6 things
you are grateful to have in your life.

1. _____
2. _____
3. _____
4. _____
5. _____
6. _____

NIGHT: Before you go to bed, write out
your manifestation statement 9 times.

1. _____
2. _____
3. _____
4. _____
5. _____
6. _____
7. _____
8. _____
9. _____

DAILY 369 METHOD

MORNING: Write your manifestation statement
3 times when you first wake up.

1. _____
2. _____
3. _____

MIDDAY: (Daily Gratitude) Write 6 things
you are grateful to have in your life.

1. _____
2. _____
3. _____
4. _____
5. _____
6. _____

NIGHT: Before you go to bed, write out
your manifestation statement 9 times.

1. _____
2. _____
3. _____
4. _____
5. _____
6. _____
7. _____
8. _____
9. _____

DAILY 369 METHOD

MORNING: Write your manifestation statement
3 times when you first wake up.

1. _____
2. _____
3. _____

MIDDAY: (Daily Gratitude) Write 6 things
you are grateful to have in your life.

1. _____
2. _____
3. _____
4. _____
5. _____
6. _____

NIGHT: Before you go to bed, write out
your manifestation statement 9 times.

1. _____
2. _____
3. _____
4. _____
5. _____
6. _____
7. _____
8. _____
9. _____

DAILY 369 METHOD

MORNING: Write your manifestation statement
3 times when you first wake up.

1. _____
2. _____
3. _____

MIDDAY: (Daily Gratitude) Write 6 things
you are grateful to have in your life.

1. _____
2. _____
3. _____
4. _____
5. _____
6. _____

NIGHT: Before you go to bed, write out
your manifestation statement 9 times.

1. _____
2. _____
3. _____
4. _____
5. _____
6. _____
7. _____
8. _____
9. _____

DAILY 369 METHOD

MORNING: Write your manifestation statement
3 times when you first wake up.

1. _____
2. _____
3. _____

MIDDAY: (Daily Gratitude) Write 6 things
you are grateful to have in your life.

1. _____
2. _____
3. _____
4. _____
5. _____
6. _____

NIGHT: Before you go to bed, write out
your manifestation statement 9 times.

1. _____
2. _____
3. _____
4. _____
5. _____
6. _____
7. _____
8. _____
9. _____

4

Meeting People Who Will Help

When the student is ready, the teacher will appear.

—Buddhist saying

Finding Your Helpers

Manifesting is a very individual, very personal process. But that doesn't mean you should go it alone. As you are manifesting your own positive energy, you'll attract others to you. These people may indeed turn out to be helpers who will bring your dream closer to you. Some people even refer to them as angels in disguise. How will you recognize these helpers? They might be people you know who are already living the life you desire. They might be people who are in a position to open doors for you. Think about people you may have met—or people you have known but are just seeing for the first time since you started manifesting. You might even think of ancestors or spiritual beings who will help you.

Are there people you could learn from? Are there people who might be able to guide you on your journey?
Use this space to write about people who might be able to help you on your path.

Helpers in Your Life

Encountering your helpers or spirit guides requires attention because you may not recognize them at first. If you are looking for a new partner, for example, you may not meet your partner directly. But you might meet the person who introduces you to your partner. You may not meet a helper in person, but, instead, you might hear them speak on a podcast, on television, or even hear a character on a scripted show speaking words that you need to hear. You may hear a message from a reading at a church service or other spiritual gathering.

Use this space to write about a time when you met someone who opened a door for you or said something that changed your direction.

Manifesting Helpful Encounters

While the laws of attraction can bring helpers to you, you can also be proactive in drawing them to you. Try this manifestation practice to attract the person you want or need at the moment.

Imagine meeting the person you need. Describe what this encounter looks like. Where will it take place? What conversation will develop? Be specific. Visualize this entire experience and write it here in present or present continuous tense.

DAILY 369 METHOD

MORNING: Write your manifestation statement
3 times when you first wake up.

1. _____
2. _____
3. _____

MIDDAY: (Daily Gratitude) Write 6 things
you are grateful to have in your life.

1. _____
2. _____
3. _____
4. _____
5. _____
6. _____

NIGHT: Before you go to bed, write out
your manifestation statement 9 times.

1. _____
2. _____
3. _____
4. _____
5. _____
6. _____
7. _____
8. _____
9. _____

DAILY 369 METHOD

MORNING: Write your manifestation statement
3 times when you first wake up.

1. _____
2. _____
3. _____

MIDDAY: (Daily Gratitude) Write 6 things
you are grateful to have in your life.

1. _____
2. _____
3. _____
4. _____
5. _____
6. _____

NIGHT: Before you go to bed, write out
your manifestation statement 9 times.

1. _____
2. _____
3. _____
4. _____
5. _____
6. _____
7. _____
8. _____
9. _____

DAILY 369 METHOD

MORNING: Write your manifestation statement
3 times when you first wake up.

1. _____
2. _____
3. _____

MIDDAY: (Daily Gratitude) Write 6 things
you are grateful to have in your life.

1. _____
2. _____
3. _____
4. _____
5. _____
6. _____

NIGHT: Before you go to bed, write out
your manifestation statement 9 times.

1. _____
2. _____
3. _____
4. _____
5. _____
6. _____
7. _____
8. _____
9. _____

DAILY 369 METHOD

MORNING: Write your manifestation statement
3 times when you first wake up.

1. _____
2. _____
3. _____

MIDDAY: (Daily Gratitude) Write 6 things
you are grateful to have in your life.

1. _____
2. _____
3. _____
4. _____
5. _____
6. _____

NIGHT: Before you go to bed, write out
your manifestation statement 9 times.

1. _____
2. _____
3. _____
4. _____
5. _____
6. _____
7. _____
8. _____
9. _____

DAILY 369 METHOD

MORNING: Write your manifestation statement
3 times when you first wake up.

1. _____
2. _____
3. _____

MIDDAY: (Daily Gratitude) Write 6 things
you are grateful to have in your life.

1. _____
2. _____
3. _____
4. _____
5. _____
6. _____

NIGHT: Before you go to bed, write out
your manifestation statement 9 times.

1. _____
2. _____
3. _____
4. _____
5. _____
6. _____
7. _____
8. _____
9. _____

DAILY 369 METHOD

MORNING: Write your manifestation statement
3 times when you first wake up.

1. _____
2. _____
3. _____

MIDDAY: (Daily Gratitude) Write 6 things
you are grateful to have in your life.

1. _____
2. _____
3. _____
4. _____
5. _____
6. _____

NIGHT: Before you go to bed, write out
your manifestation statement 9 times.

1. _____
2. _____
3. _____
4. _____
5. _____
6. _____
7. _____
8. _____
9. _____

DAILY 369 METHOD

MORNING: Write your manifestation statement
3 times when you first wake up.

1. _____
2. _____
3. _____

MIDDAY: (Daily Gratitude) Write 6 things
you are grateful to have in your life.

1. _____
2. _____
3. _____
4. _____
5. _____
6. _____

NIGHT: Before you go to bed, write out
your manifestation statement 9 times.

1. _____
2. _____
3. _____
4. _____
5. _____
6. _____
7. _____
8. _____
9. _____

DAILY 369 METHOD

MORNING: Write your manifestation statement
3 times when you first wake up.

1. _____
2. _____
3. _____

MIDDAY: (Daily Gratitude) Write 6 things
you are grateful to have in your life.

1. _____
2. _____
3. _____
4. _____
5. _____
6. _____

NIGHT: Before you go to bed, write out
your manifestation statement 9 times.

1. _____
2. _____
3. _____
4. _____
5. _____
6. _____
7. _____
8. _____
9. _____

5

Letting Go of Limiting Beliefs

If you accept
a limiting
belief, then
it will
become a
truth for you.

—Louise Hay

You, Unlimited

A limiting belief is a belief or judgement you have about yourself that holds you back. We all have them. We might believe that we are not good enough, smart enough, or attractive enough to get what we want. But these are the very thoughts that will keep us from manifesting our dreams. Truly letting go of these thoughts is absolutely essential to achieving success.

Use the space on these pages to write out as many limiting beliefs about yourself as come to mind. The more you acknowledge them, the easier it will be to eliminate them from your life.

Releasing Negative Energy

You no longer need those limiting beliefs. It is time for you to put them behind you. Some people find it helpful to thank the belief for how it may have protected them in the past. You may choose to do so here. Here you will commit to giving yourself permission to move beyond these beliefs.

Use the space below to write the following permission statement to yourself as many times as it takes for you to start embodying it. Do this for each limiting belief.

Example: I give myself permission to stop believing that I am not attractive enough to be loved.

Writing a New Story

Now that you've let go of those limiting beliefs, it's time to write a new story. Use the language of affirmation (I am instead of I will be). Use the space below to record beliefs about yourself that will fill you with energy.

DAILY 369 METHOD

MORNING: Write your manifestation statement
3 times when you first wake up.

1. _____
2. _____
3. _____

MIDDAY: (Daily Gratitude) Write 6 things
you are grateful to have in your life.

1. _____
2. _____
3. _____
4. _____
5. _____
6. _____

NIGHT: Before you go to bed, write out
your manifestation statement 9 times.

1. _____
2. _____
3. _____
4. _____
5. _____
6. _____
7. _____
8. _____
9. _____

DAILY 369 METHOD

MORNING: Write your manifestation statement
3 times when you first wake up.

1. _____
2. _____
3. _____

MIDDAY: (Daily Gratitude) Write 6 things
you are grateful to have in your life.

1. _____
2. _____
3. _____
4. _____
5. _____
6. _____

NIGHT: Before you go to bed, write out
your manifestation statement 9 times.

1. _____
2. _____
3. _____
4. _____
5. _____
6. _____
7. _____
8. _____
9. _____

DAILY 369 METHOD

MORNING: Write your manifestation statement
3 times when you first wake up.

1. _____
2. _____
3. _____

MIDDAY: (Daily Gratitude) Write 6 things
you are grateful to have in your life.

1. _____
2. _____
3. _____
4. _____
5. _____
6. _____

NIGHT: Before you go to bed, write out
your manifestation statement 9 times.

1. _____
2. _____
3. _____
4. _____
5. _____
6. _____
7. _____
8. _____
9. _____

DAILY 369 METHOD

MORNING: Write your manifestation statement
3 times when you first wake up.

1. _____
2. _____
3. _____

MIDDAY: (Daily Gratitude) Write 6 things
you are grateful to have in your life.

1. _____
2. _____
3. _____
4. _____
5. _____
6. _____

NIGHT: Before you go to bed, write out
your manifestation statement 9 times.

1. _____
2. _____
3. _____
4. _____
5. _____
6. _____
7. _____
8. _____
9. _____

DAILY 369 METHOD

MORNING: Write your manifestation statement
3 times when you first wake up.

1. _____
2. _____
3. _____

MIDDAY: (Daily Gratitude) Write 6 things
you are grateful to have in your life.

1. _____
2. _____
3. _____
4. _____
5. _____
6. _____

NIGHT: Before you go to bed, write out
your manifestation statement 9 times.

1. _____
2. _____
3. _____
4. _____
5. _____
6. _____
7. _____
8. _____
9. _____

DAILY 369 METHOD

MORNING: Write your manifestation statement
3 times when you first wake up.

1. _____
2. _____
3. _____

MIDDAY: (Daily Gratitude) Write 6 things
you are grateful to have in your life.

1. _____
2. _____
3. _____
4. _____
5. _____
6. _____

NIGHT: Before you go to bed, write out
your manifestation statement 9 times.

1. _____
2. _____
3. _____
4. _____
5. _____
6. _____
7. _____
8. _____
9. _____

DAILY 369 METHOD

MORNING: Write your manifestation statement
3 times when you first wake up.

1. _____
2. _____
3. _____

MIDDAY: (Daily Gratitude) Write 6 things
you are grateful to have in your life.

1. _____
2. _____
3. _____
4. _____
5. _____
6. _____

NIGHT: Before you go to bed, write out
your manifestation statement 9 times.

1. _____
2. _____
3. _____
4. _____
5. _____
6. _____
7. _____
8. _____
9. _____

DAILY 369 METHOD

MORNING: Write your manifestation statement
3 times when you first wake up.

1. _____
2. _____
3. _____

MIDDAY: (Daily Gratitude) Write 6 things
you are grateful to have in your life.

1. _____
2. _____
3. _____
4. _____
5. _____
6. _____

NIGHT: Before you go to bed, write out
your manifestation statement 9 times.

1. _____
2. _____
3. _____
4. _____
5. _____
6. _____
7. _____
8. _____
9. _____

6

Expressing Gratitude

Be thankful
for what you
have, you'll
end up having
more. If you
concentrate
on what you
don't have,
you will never
ever have
enough.

– Oprah Winfrey

So Much to Be Grateful For

Gratitude is essential to manifesting. It helps to build the positive energy you need to achieve your dreams. What do you have to be grateful for? A lot! Spend some time really thinking about what you already have. It can be anything from friendship to a warm place to sleep at night. In fact, your life is already complete, even before you receive what you are manifesting. When you have gratitude, your vibrational energy soars. You become aligned with your desires.

Use the space on these pages to record as many things that you're grateful for as possible. Start each statement with "I'm grateful for..."

Embracing Abundance

When you are grateful, your negative thoughts begin to vanish. With them, your negative energy also begins to vanish. Instead of longing, you'll be filled with a sense of abundance. That's a key part of changing your energy and mindset, important parts of the process of manifesting. Consider all that you are grateful for. Imagine yourself surrounded by abundance.

Use the space below to write about the feeling of being surrounded by abundance. Make sure to include the feeling of worthiness and gratitude you have for this abundance.

DAILY 369 METHOD

MORNING: Write your manifestation statement
3 times when you first wake up.

1. _____
2. _____
3. _____

MIDDAY: (Daily Gratitude) Write 6 things
you are grateful to have in your life.

1. _____
2. _____
3. _____
4. _____
5. _____
6. _____

NIGHT: Before you go to bed, write out
your manifestation statement 9 times.

1. _____
2. _____
3. _____
4. _____
5. _____
6. _____
7. _____
8. _____
9. _____

DAILY 369 METHOD

MORNING: Write your manifestation statement
3 times when you first wake up.

1. _____
2. _____
3. _____

MIDDAY: (Daily Gratitude) Write 6 things
you are grateful to have in your life.

1. _____
2. _____
3. _____
4. _____
5. _____
6. _____

NIGHT: Before you go to bed, write out
your manifestation statement 9 times.

1. _____
2. _____
3. _____
4. _____
5. _____
6. _____
7. _____
8. _____
9. _____

DAILY **369** METHOD

MORNING: Write your manifestation statement
3 times when you first wake up.

1. _____
2. _____
3. _____

MIDDAY: (Daily Gratitude) Write 6 things
you are grateful to have in your life.

1. _____
2. _____
3. _____
4. _____
5. _____
6. _____

NIGHT: Before you go to bed, write out
your manifestation statement 9 times.

1. _____
2. _____
3. _____
4. _____
5. _____
6. _____
7. _____
8. _____
9. _____

DAILY 369 METHOD

MORNING: Write your manifestation statement
3 times when you first wake up.

1. _____
2. _____
3. _____

MIDDAY: (Daily Gratitude) Write 6 things
you are grateful to have in your life.

1. _____
2. _____
3. _____
4. _____
5. _____
6. _____

NIGHT: Before you go to bed, write out
your manifestation statement 9 times.

1. _____
2. _____
3. _____
4. _____
5. _____
6. _____
7. _____
8. _____
9. _____

DAILY 369 METHOD

MORNING: Write your manifestation statement
3 times when you first wake up.

1. _____
2. _____
3. _____

MIDDAY: (Daily Gratitude) Write 6 things
you are grateful to have in your life.

1. _____
2. _____
3. _____
4. _____
5. _____
6. _____

NIGHT: Before you go to bed, write out
your manifestation statement 9 times.

1. _____
2. _____
3. _____
4. _____
5. _____
6. _____
7. _____
8. _____
9. _____

DAILY 369 METHOD

MORNING: Write your manifestation statement
3 times when you first wake up.

1. _____
2. _____
3. _____

MIDDAY: (Daily Gratitude) Write 6 things
you are grateful to have in your life.

1. _____
2. _____
3. _____
4. _____
5. _____
6. _____

NIGHT: Before you go to bed, write out
your manifestation statement 9 times.

1. _____
2. _____
3. _____
4. _____
5. _____
6. _____
7. _____
8. _____
9. _____

DAILY 369 METHOD

MORNING: Write your manifestation statement
3 times when you first wake up.

1. _____
2. _____
3. _____

MIDDAY: (Daily Gratitude) Write 6 things
you are grateful to have in your life.

1. _____
2. _____
3. _____
4. _____
5. _____
6. _____

NIGHT: Before you go to bed, write out
your manifestation statement 9 times.

1. _____
2. _____
3. _____
4. _____
5. _____
6. _____
7. _____
8. _____
9. _____

7

Embodying Positive Energy

Focus on
an ocean of
positives, not
a puddle of
negatives.

—Kevin Ansbro

Embodying Positive Energy

The law of attraction centers on the allocation of energy. You know that in order for your affirmations to produce the change you seek, you must believe. You must embody the energy of these affirmations. For some, truly believing and embodying is the hardest part. Their thoughts are not aligned with their bodies. While the mind struggles to believe, the body holds on to old negative patterns and energy. Changing that takes practice.

Try doing a body scan to find out where you might be holding onto negative energy. Start at your feet. Are they tired or tingly? Moving up your legs, do you feel creaky or stiff? In each spot send that part of your body positive thoughts. Use visualization to imagine that area being flooded with health-giving vibrations.

After you've tried it, record your experience here. Write down what parts of your body you think might be holding on to negative energy.

Releasing Self-Doubt

As you've continued with your affirmations, you have increased your positive energy and are continuing to draw your desires toward you. But it's normal for doubts to sneak in some times. Try this exercise to release your doubts.

- Close your eyes and center on your breathing.

- Slow your breath.

- Become aware of what you're feeling as you scan your body.

- Wrap your arms around yourself.

- Become aware of the sensation of security you have.

- You are being held and you are safe.

- Realize that it is your own strength that is holding you.

- Be grateful for your inner strength.

- Realize that you can trust yourself.

- You are enough.

Being Generous with Yourself and Others

Generosity is an extension of gratitude. When we are grateful, we can be generous because we have so much to give. You can be generous in many ways—with time, with money, with attention, and more. When you give, you manifest positive energy. You can give to others, but you can also practice gratitude with yourself.

Use the space below to record some of the ways you've been generous with yourself or others lately. Did you allow yourself the sleep you need? Did you mentor someone who needed help? As you give, you manifest positive energy.

DAILY **369** METHOD

MORNING: Write your manifestation statement
3 times when you first wake up.

1. _____
2. _____
3. _____

MIDDAY: (Daily Gratitude) Write 6 things
you are grateful to have in your life.

1. _____
2. _____
3. _____
4. _____
5. _____
6. _____

NIGHT: Before you go to bed, write out
your manifestation statement 9 times.

1. _____
2. _____
3. _____
4. _____
5. _____
6. _____
7. _____
8. _____
9. _____

DAILY 369 METHOD

MORNING: Write your manifestation statement
3 times when you first wake up.

1. _____
2. _____
3. _____

MIDDAY: (Daily Gratitude) Write 6 things
you are grateful to have in your life.

1. _____
2. _____
3. _____
4. _____
5. _____
6. _____

NIGHT: Before you go to bed, write out
your manifestation statement 9 times.

1. _____
2. _____
3. _____
4. _____
5. _____
6. _____
7. _____
8. _____
9. _____

DAILY 369 METHOD

MORNING: Write your manifestation statement
3 times when you first wake up.

1. _____
2. _____
3. _____

MIDDAY: (Daily Gratitude) Write 6 things
you are grateful to have in your life.

1. _____
2. _____
3. _____
4. _____
5. _____
6. _____

NIGHT: Before you go to bed, write out
your manifestation statement 9 times.

1. _____
2. _____
3. _____
4. _____
5. _____
6. _____
7. _____
8. _____
9. _____

DAILY 369 METHOD

MORNING: Write your manifestation statement
3 times when you first wake up.

1. _____
2. _____
3. _____

MIDDAY: (Daily Gratitude) Write 6 things
you are grateful to have in your life.

1. _____
2. _____
3. _____
4. _____
5. _____
6. _____

NIGHT: Before you go to bed, write out
your manifestation statement 9 times.

1. _____
2. _____
3. _____
4. _____
5. _____
6. _____
7. _____
8. _____
9. _____

DAILY 369 METHOD

MORNING: Write your manifestation statement
3 times when you first wake up.

1. _____
2. _____
3. _____

MIDDAY: (Daily Gratitude) Write 6 things
you are grateful to have in your life.

1. _____
2. _____
3. _____
4. _____
5. _____
6. _____

NIGHT: Before you go to bed, write out
your manifestation statement 9 times.

1. _____
2. _____
3. _____
4. _____
5. _____
6. _____
7. _____
8. _____
9. _____

DAILY 369 METHOD

MORNING: Write your manifestation statement
3 times when you first wake up.

1. _____
2. _____
3. _____

MIDDAY: (Daily Gratitude) Write 6 things
you are grateful to have in your life.

1. _____
2. _____
3. _____
4. _____
5. _____
6. _____

NIGHT: Before you go to bed, write out
your manifestation statement 9 times.

1. _____
2. _____
3. _____
4. _____
5. _____
6. _____
7. _____
8. _____
9. _____

DAILY 369 METHOD

MORNING: Write your manifestation statement
3 times when you first wake up.

1. _____
2. _____
3. _____

MIDDAY: (Daily Gratitude) Write 6 things
you are grateful to have in your life.

1. _____
2. _____
3. _____
4. _____
5. _____
6. _____

NIGHT: Before you go to bed, write out
your manifestation statement 9 times.

1. _____
2. _____
3. _____
4. _____
5. _____
6. _____
7. _____
8. _____
9. _____

8

Aligning Your Vibrations

Be the
energy
you want
to
attract.

—Anonymous

Universal Vibrations

Your energy is channeled through your intentions. When you live and breathe your intentions as you are now doing, your intentions will create vibrations. These vibrations are your signal to the universe. When they are vibrant and positive, they will signal to the universe that you are ready to receive your desires. You must assume that it is a given: you will receive. This inevitability will fill you will happiness and ease.

To align yourself with the gifts of the universe, try imagining all the positive energy that surrounds you. Now imagine yourself as part of this. Acknowledge that you are an important part of the universe. You are not separate. Now imagine those infinite gifts—that belong to you, that you are a part of—are there for you to enjoy. How does it feel to know that so much abundance is there for you?

Write about your feelings as you imagine your rightful place in the universe and your ability to embody its energy and gifts.

Visualizing Your Alignment

At each step on your journey, you can use all the tools of manifestation that you've learned about so far. Just because you've visualized your success once doesn't mean you're finished. Visualization is a powerful tool for alignment.

Visualize the energy radiating out of you. What does it look like? Does it have a color? A sound? Is it warm or cool? Now picture this energy encountering the beautiful, harmonious energy of the universe. Picture your energy intermingling with the most powerful energy in the universe and drawing it to you. What does it feel like when you realize you have drawn this energy into your life?

Write down your feelings and realize that this is what you are doing when you manifest.

_____

_____

_____

_____

_____

_____

_____

_____

_____

_____

_____

_____

Getting into Flow

Have you heard the expression 'being in a flow state?' It's used to describe the feeling when everything seems to click—you feel a sense of ease in your life, as if everything comes naturally to you. You don't have to force anything. Alignment is another way to think about flow. Here's another way to visualize this state.

You wake up in the morning feeling both excited and at peace. The day ahead holds only good things for you. You are filled with gratitude for your health, your surroundings, and your relationships. Serendipitous encounters bring you help and happiness throughout the day. You can manifest this reality.

Use this space to describe what a perfect day in your 'flow state' would look like. Make sure to use present tense and details you experience from all your senses.

_____

_____

_____

_____

_____

_____

_____

_____

_____

_____

_____

DAILY 369 METHOD

MORNING: Write your manifestation statement
3 times when you first wake up.

1. _____
2. _____
3. _____

MIDDAY: (Daily Gratitude) Write 6 things
you are grateful to have in your life.

1. _____
2. _____
3. _____
4. _____
5. _____
6. _____

NIGHT: Before you go to bed, write out
your manifestation statement 9 times.

1. _____
2. _____
3. _____
4. _____
5. _____
6. _____
7. _____
8. _____
9. _____

DAILY 369 METHOD

MORNING: Write your manifestation statement
3 times when you first wake up.

1. _____
2. _____
3. _____

MIDDAY: (Daily Gratitude) Write 6 things
you are grateful to have in your life.

1. _____
2. _____
3. _____
4. _____
5. _____
6. _____

NIGHT: Before you go to bed, write out
your manifestation statement 9 times.

1. _____
2. _____
3. _____
4. _____
5. _____
6. _____
7. _____
8. _____
9. _____

DAILY 369 METHOD

MORNING: Write your manifestation statement
3 times when you first wake up.

1. _____
2. _____
3. _____

MIDDAY: (Daily Gratitude) Write 6 things
you are grateful to have in your life.

1. _____
2. _____
3. _____
4. _____
5. _____
6. _____

NIGHT: Before you go to bed, write out
your manifestation statement 9 times.

1. _____
2. _____
3. _____
4. _____
5. _____
6. _____
7. _____
8. _____
9. _____

DAILY **369** METHOD

MORNING: Write your manifestation statement
3 times when you first wake up.

1. _____
2. _____
3. _____

MIDDAY: (Daily Gratitude) Write 6 things
you are grateful to have in your life.

1. _____
2. _____
3. _____
4. _____
5. _____
6. _____

NIGHT: Before you go to bed, write out
your manifestation statement 9 times.

1. _____
2. _____
3. _____
4. _____
5. _____
6. _____
7. _____
8. _____
9. _____

DAILY 369 METHOD

MORNING: Write your manifestation statement
3 times when you first wake up.

1. _____
2. _____
3. _____

MIDDAY: (Daily Gratitude) Write 6 things
you are grateful to have in your life.

1. _____
2. _____
3. _____
4. _____
5. _____
6. _____

NIGHT: Before you go to bed, write out
your manifestation statement 9 times.

1. _____
2. _____
3. _____
4. _____
5. _____
6. _____
7. _____
8. _____
9. _____

DAILY 369 METHOD

MORNING: Write your manifestation statement
3 times when you first wake up.

1. _____
2. _____
3. _____

MIDDAY: (Daily Gratitude) Write 6 things
you are grateful to have in your life.

1. _____
2. _____
3. _____
4. _____
5. _____
6. _____

NIGHT: Before you go to bed, write out
your manifestation statement 9 times.

1. _____
2. _____
3. _____
4. _____
5. _____
6. _____
7. _____
8. _____
9. _____

DAILY 369 METHOD

MORNING: Write your manifestation statement
3 times when you first wake up.

1. _____
2. _____
3. _____

MIDDAY: (Daily Gratitude) Write 6 things
you are grateful to have in your life.

1. _____
2. _____
3. _____
4. _____
5. _____
6. _____

NIGHT: Before you go to bed, write out
your manifestation statement 9 times.

1. _____
2. _____
3. _____
4. _____
5. _____
6. _____
7. _____
8. _____
9. _____

DAILY 369 METHOD

MORNING: Write your manifestation statement
3 times when you first wake up.

1. _____
2. _____
3. _____

MIDDAY: (Daily Gratitude) Write 6 things
you are grateful to have in your life.

1. _____
2. _____
3. _____
4. _____
5. _____
6. _____

NIGHT: Before you go to bed, write out
your manifestation statement 9 times.

1. _____
2. _____
3. _____
4. _____
5. _____
6. _____
7. _____
8. _____
9. _____

9

Practice Trust

Embrace the uncertainty of becoming. When nothing is certain, anything is possible.

— Mandy Hale

Focus on Belief

For some, one of the most difficult parts of manifesting is trusting the process. How do you know that your dreams are on their way to you? The answer is that you must believe, and you must trust. That can be easier said than done. You may have had negative experiences in the past. It may be hard for you to let go of your self-protection. Try this exercise for amplifying your trust.

Think of times in the past when your experiences have caused you to lose faith in people and in yourself. Now let go of these experiences. You can start by writing "I let go of..." below.

For example:

- I let go of the distrust I developed because I had my heart broken.

- I let go of my distrust in love because of my parents' break up.

- I let go of distrust in my own worth because I was undervalued at my last job.

Use the space on these pages to let go.

Revisiting Affirmations

To manifest, you must believe in something you don't always see right away—that your dreams, although they haven't arrived yet— are on their way. Affirmations can help you to increase your belief.

Examples:

- My dreams are on the way to me.
- I know my manifestation is working.
- I can feel my dreams coming to me.

For these affirmations to work, you must truly believe. Use this space to write affirmations about your trust in the process.

DAILY 369 METHOD

MORNING: Write your manifestation statement
3 times when you first wake up.

1. _____
2. _____
3. _____

MIDDAY: (Daily Gratitude) Write 6 things
you are grateful to have in your life.

1. _____
2. _____
3. _____
4. _____
5. _____
6. _____

NIGHT: Before you go to bed, write out
your manifestation statement 9 times.

1. _____
2. _____
3. _____
4. _____
5. _____
6. _____
7. _____
8. _____
9. _____

DAILY 369 METHOD

MORNING: Write your manifestation statement
3 times when you first wake up.

1. _____
2. _____
3. _____

MIDDAY: (Daily Gratitude) Write 6 things
you are grateful to have in your life.

1. _____
2. _____
3. _____
4. _____
5. _____
6. _____

NIGHT: Before you go to bed, write out
your manifestation statement 9 times.

1. _____
2. _____
3. _____
4. _____
5. _____
6. _____
7. _____
8. _____
9. _____

DAILY 369 METHOD

MORNING: Write your manifestation statement
3 times when you first wake up.

1. _____
2. _____
3. _____

MIDDAY: (Daily Gratitude) Write 6 things
you are grateful to have in your life.

1. _____
2. _____
3. _____
4. _____
5. _____
6. _____

NIGHT: Before you go to bed, write out
your manifestation statement 9 times.

1. _____
2. _____
3. _____
4. _____
5. _____
6. _____
7. _____
8. _____
9. _____

DAILY 369 METHOD

MORNING: Write your manifestation statement
3 times when you first wake up.

1. _____
2. _____
3. _____

MIDDAY: (Daily Gratitude) Write 6 things
you are grateful to have in your life.

1. _____
2. _____
3. _____
4. _____
5. _____
6. _____

NIGHT: Before you go to bed, write out
your manifestation statement 9 times.

1. _____
2. _____
3. _____
4. _____
5. _____
6. _____
7. _____
8. _____
9. _____

DAILY 369 METHOD

MORNING: Write your manifestation statement
3 times when you first wake up.

1. _____
2. _____
3. _____

MIDDAY: (Daily Gratitude) Write 6 things
you are grateful to have in your life.

1. _____
2. _____
3. _____
4. _____
5. _____
6. _____

NIGHT: Before you go to bed, write out
your manifestation statement 9 times.

1. _____
2. _____
3. _____
4. _____
5. _____
6. _____
7. _____
8. _____
9. _____

DAILY 369 METHOD

MORNING: Write your manifestation statement
3 times when you first wake up.

1. _____
2. _____
3. _____

MIDDAY: (Daily Gratitude) Write 6 things
you are grateful to have in your life.

1. _____
2. _____
3. _____
4. _____
5. _____
6. _____

NIGHT: Before you go to bed, write out
your manifestation statement 9 times.

1. _____
2. _____
3. _____
4. _____
5. _____
6. _____
7. _____
8. _____
9. _____

DAILY 369 METHOD

MORNING: Write your manifestation statement
3 times when you first wake up.

1. _____
2. _____
3. _____

MIDDAY: (Daily Gratitude) Write 6 things
you are grateful to have in your life.

1. _____
2. _____
3. _____
4. _____
5. _____
6. _____

NIGHT: Before you go to bed, write out
your manifestation statement 9 times.

1. _____
2. _____
3. _____
4. _____
5. _____
6. _____
7. _____
8. _____
9. _____

10

Experiencing Connection

If you want
to find the
secrets of
the universe,
think in terms
of energy,
frequency,
and vibration."

— Nikola Tesla

Channeling Energy

By now you're starting to recognize the connection between the energy you are putting out and the results you are getting back. What does that feel like?

Use the space below to describe in sensory detail how you feel your energy has changed. What feels different? What vibrations are you feeling now that weren't there before?

Use this space to explain how your energy is connecting to the positive energy in the universe. What ways have you seen your energy attracting positivity since you started manifesting?

Connections and Vibrations

Manifesting helps you to see new paths that you couldn't see before. Describe some of the paths and connections that have appeared to you and how you recognized them as signs that your dream is on its way.

DAILY 369 METHOD

MORNING: Write your manifestation statement
3 times when you first wake up.

1. _____
2. _____
3. _____

MIDDAY: (Daily Gratitude) Write 6 things
you are grateful to have in your life.

1. _____
2. _____
3. _____
4. _____
5. _____
6. _____

NIGHT: Before you go to bed, write out
your manifestation statement 9 times.

1. _____
2. _____
3. _____
4. _____
5. _____
6. _____
7. _____
8. _____
9. _____

DAILY 369 METHOD

MORNING: Write your manifestation statement
3 times when you first wake up.

1. _____
2. _____
3. _____

MIDDAY: (Daily Gratitude) Write 6 things
you are grateful to have in your life.

1. _____
2. _____
3. _____
4. _____
5. _____
6. _____

NIGHT: Before you go to bed, write out
your manifestation statement 9 times.

1. _____
2. _____
3. _____
4. _____
5. _____
6. _____
7. _____
8. _____
9. _____

DAILY 369 METHOD

MORNING: Write your manifestation statement
3 times when you first wake up.

1. _____
2. _____
3. _____

MIDDAY: (Daily Gratitude) Write 6 things
you are grateful to have in your life.

1. _____
2. _____
3. _____
4. _____
5. _____
6. _____

NIGHT: Before you go to bed, write out
your manifestation statement 9 times.

1. _____
2. _____
3. _____
4. _____
5. _____
6. _____
7. _____
8. _____
9. _____

DAILY **369** METHOD

MORNING: Write your manifestation statement
3 times when you first wake up.

1. _____
2. _____
3. _____

MIDDAY: (Daily Gratitude) Write 6 things
you are grateful to have in your life.

1. _____
2. _____
3. _____
4. _____
5. _____
6. _____

NIGHT: Before you go to bed, write out
your manifestation statement 9 times.

1. _____
2. _____
3. _____
4. _____
5. _____
6. _____
7. _____
8. _____
9. _____

DAILY 369 METHOD

MORNING: Write your manifestation statement
3 times when you first wake up.

1. _____
2. _____
3. _____

MIDDAY: (Daily Gratitude) Write 6 things
you are grateful to have in your life.

1. _____
2. _____
3. _____
4. _____
5. _____
6. _____

NIGHT: Before you go to bed, write out
your manifestation statement 9 times.

1. _____
2. _____
3. _____
4. _____
5. _____
6. _____
7. _____
8. _____
9. _____

DAILY 369 METHOD

MORNING: Write your manifestation statement
3 times when you first wake up.

1. _____
2. _____
3. _____

MIDDAY: (Daily Gratitude) Write 6 things
you are grateful to have in your life.

1. _____
2. _____
3. _____
4. _____
5. _____
6. _____

NIGHT: Before you go to bed, write out
your manifestation statement 9 times.

1. _____
2. _____
3. _____
4. _____
5. _____
6. _____
7. _____
8. _____
9. _____

DAILY 369 METHOD

MORNING: Write your manifestation statement
3 times when you first wake up.

1. _____
2. _____
3. _____

MIDDAY: (Daily Gratitude) Write 6 things
you are grateful to have in your life.

1. _____
2. _____
3. _____
4. _____
5. _____
6. _____

NIGHT: Before you go to bed, write out
your manifestation statement 9 times.

1. _____
2. _____
3. _____
4. _____
5. _____
6. _____
7. _____
8. _____
9. _____

11

Seeking Serendipity

Sometimes serendipity is just intention unmasked.

—Elizabeth Berg

Beyond Coincidence

You've been doing the work. You've been manifesting positive energy. Good things are starting to happen. Events are taking place that are getting you closer to your goals. People are coming into your life. You're starting to see serendipity. What is serendipity? It's the alignment of your energy with opportunities that get you closer to your dreams. Now that your energy is more aligned, you can see these opportunities as never before.

Use the space below to write about experiences that have happened since you started manifesting that prove to you that your process is working.

_____

_____

_____

_____

_____

_____

_____

_____

_____

_____

_____

_____

_____

_____

_____

_____

Your intention is creating serendipity for you. Use the space below to write about a 'happy coincidence' that took place since you've been manifesting. Did you just happen to run into someone who could help you with your career? Did your new energy attract the right person to you?

The Universe is Responding

Think about something good that has happened to you since you started manifesting. Write about it here. Do you think it was just a coincidence or the result of serendipity?

Write your thoughts about it here.

_____

_____

_____

_____

_____

_____

_____

_____

_____

_____

_____

_____

_____

_____

_____

_____

_____

_____

_____

_____

_____

_____

DAILY 369 METHOD

MORNING: Write your manifestation statement
3 times when you first wake up.

1. _____
2. _____
3. _____

MIDDAY: (Daily Gratitude) Write 6 things
you are grateful to have in your life.

1. _____
2. _____
3. _____
4. _____
5. _____
6. _____

NIGHT: Before you go to bed, write out
your manifestation statement 9 times.

1. _____
2. _____
3. _____
4. _____
5. _____
6. _____
7. _____
8. _____
9. _____

DAILY 369 METHOD

MORNING: Write your manifestation statement
3 times when you first wake up.

1. _____
2. _____
3. _____

MIDDAY: (Daily Gratitude) Write 6 things
you are grateful to have in your life.

1. _____
2. _____
3. _____
4. _____
5. _____
6. _____

NIGHT: Before you go to bed, write out
your manifestation statement 9 times.

1. _____
2. _____
3. _____
4. _____
5. _____
6. _____
7. _____
8. _____
9. _____

DAILY 369 METHOD

MORNING: Write your manifestation statement
3 times when you first wake up.

1. _____
2. _____
3. _____

MIDDAY: (Daily Gratitude) Write 6 things
you are grateful to have in your life.

1. _____
2. _____
3. _____
4. _____
5. _____
6. _____

NIGHT: Before you go to bed, write out
your manifestation statement 9 times.

1. _____
2. _____
3. _____
4. _____
5. _____
6. _____
7. _____
8. _____
9. _____

DAILY 369 METHOD

MORNING: Write your manifestation statement
3 times when you first wake up.

1. _____
2. _____
3. _____

MIDDAY: (Daily Gratitude) Write 6 things
you are grateful to have in your life.

1. _____
2. _____
3. _____
4. _____
5. _____
6. _____

NIGHT: Before you go to bed, write out
your manifestation statement 9 times.

1. _____
2. _____
3. _____
4. _____
5. _____
6. _____
7. _____
8. _____
9. _____

DAILY **369** METHOD

MORNING: Write your manifestation statement
3 times when you first wake up.

1. _____
2. _____
3. _____

MIDDAY: (Daily Gratitude) Write 6 things
you are grateful to have in your life.

1. _____
2. _____
3. _____
4. _____
5. _____
6. _____

NIGHT: Before you go to bed, write out
your manifestation statement 9 times.

1. _____
2. _____
3. _____
4. _____
5. _____
6. _____
7. _____
8. _____
9. _____

DAILY 369 METHOD

MORNING: Write your manifestation statement
3 times when you first wake up.

1. _____
2. _____
3. _____

MIDDAY: (Daily Gratitude) Write 6 things
you are grateful to have in your life.

1. _____
2. _____
3. _____
4. _____
5. _____
6. _____

NIGHT: Before you go to bed, write out
your manifestation statement 9 times.

1. _____
2. _____
3. _____
4. _____
5. _____
6. _____
7. _____
8. _____
9. _____

DAILY 369 METHOD

MORNING: Write your manifestation statement
3 times when you first wake up.

1. _____
2. _____
3. _____

MIDDAY: (Daily Gratitude) Write 6 things
you are grateful to have in your life.

1. _____
2. _____
3. _____
4. _____
5. _____
6. _____

NIGHT: Before you go to bed, write out
your manifestation statement 9 times.

1. _____
2. _____
3. _____
4. _____
5. _____
6. _____
7. _____
8. _____
9. _____

12

Believing in Your Worth

Once we believe
in ourselves,
we can risk
curiosity, wonder,
spontaneous
delight or any
experience
that reveals the
human spirit.

—E.E. Cummings

Transformation is Happening

Truly believing you are worthy can be one of the hardest parts of manifesting. Some might create and repeat affirmations about self-worth, but not genuinely believe. Use this space to write about experiences that help you feel worthy. Think about ways you have recently surprised yourself. Have you recently done something the old you would have never been able to do?

Write about how you are able to see a recent development in your life as a sign that you have been transformed.

Use this space to create affirmations about your worthiness to receive what you manifest. Be bold. Be confident. Truly believe what you're writing. Repeat the affirmations as many times as it takes for you to be able to believe.

I am Worthy

You have now arrived at the point where you truly believe in your worthiness. You believe you deserve to receive what you desire.

Use this space to describe the positive feelings and vibrations that course through you when you accept this truth.

DAILY 369 METHOD

MORNING: Write your manifestation statement
3 times when you first wake up.

1. _____
2. _____
3. _____

MIDDAY: (Daily Gratitude) Write 6 things
you are grateful to have in your life.

1. _____
2. _____
3. _____
4. _____
5. _____
6. _____

NIGHT: Before you go to bed, write out
your manifestation statement 9 times.

1. _____
2. _____
3. _____
4. _____
5. _____
6. _____
7. _____
8. _____
9. _____

DAILY 369 METHOD

MORNING: Write your manifestation statement
3 times when you first wake up.

1. _____
2. _____
3. _____

MIDDAY: (Daily Gratitude) Write 6 things
you are grateful to have in your life.

1. _____
2. _____
3. _____
4. _____
5. _____
6. _____

NIGHT: Before you go to bed, write out
your manifestation statement 9 times.

1. _____
2. _____
3. _____
4. _____
5. _____
6. _____
7. _____
8. _____
9. _____

DAILY 369 METHOD

MORNING: Write your manifestation statement
3 times when you first wake up.

1. _____
2. _____
3. _____

MIDDAY: (Daily Gratitude) Write 6 things
you are grateful to have in your life.

1. _____
2. _____
3. _____
4. _____
5. _____
6. _____

NIGHT: Before you go to bed, write out
your manifestation statement 9 times.

1. _____
2. _____
3. _____
4. _____
5. _____
6. _____
7. _____
8. _____
9. _____

DAILY 369 METHOD

MORNING: Write your manifestation statement
3 times when you first wake up.

1. _____
2. _____
3. _____

MIDDAY: (Daily Gratitude) Write 6 things
you are grateful to have in your life.

1. _____
2. _____
3. _____
4. _____
5. _____
6. _____

NIGHT: Before you go to bed, write out
your manifestation statement 9 times.

1. _____
2. _____
3. _____
4. _____
5. _____
6. _____
7. _____
8. _____
9. _____

DAILY 369 METHOD

MORNING: Write your manifestation statement
3 times when you first wake up.

1. _____
2. _____
3. _____

MIDDAY: (Daily Gratitude) Write 6 things
you are grateful to have in your life.

1. _____
2. _____
3. _____
4. _____
5. _____
6. _____

NIGHT: Before you go to bed, write out
your manifestation statement 9 times.

1. _____
2. _____
3. _____
4. _____
5. _____
6. _____
7. _____
8. _____
9. _____

DAILY 369 METHOD

MORNING: Write your manifestation statement
3 times when you first wake up.

1. _____
2. _____
3. _____

MIDDAY: (Daily Gratitude) Write 6 things
you are grateful to have in your life.

1. _____
2. _____
3. _____
4. _____
5. _____
6. _____

NIGHT: Before you go to bed, write out
your manifestation statement 9 times.

1. _____
2. _____
3. _____
4. _____
5. _____
6. _____
7. _____
8. _____
9. _____

DAILY 369 METHOD

MORNING: Write your manifestation statement
3 times when you first wake up.

1. _____
2. _____
3. _____

MIDDAY: (Daily Gratitude) Write 6 things
you are grateful to have in your life.

1. _____
2. _____
3. _____
4. _____
5. _____
6. _____

NIGHT: Before you go to bed, write out
your manifestation statement 9 times.

1. _____
2. _____
3. _____
4. _____
5. _____
6. _____
7. _____
8. _____
9. _____

13

Dreams
Delivered

Success
will be within
your reach
only when
you start
reaching out
for it.

—Stephen Richards

Getting Ready to Receive

Are you ready to receive what you manifested? Some call this being in 'receiving mode.' What does that look like? It's all about being open and accepting and truly believing that you deserve your dreams. Are you willing to receive help? Are you willing to receive compliments?

Use this space to write affirmations that express that you are willing to receive.

Your Manifestation is Almost Here

When your manifestation is close to arriving, you'll see signs. If you are manifesting money, perhaps you start to see dropped coins along your path as you walk. If you are manifesting a healthier life, perhaps you begin to hear song lyrics about feeling good. Pay attention and you'll begin to see signs around you.

Use this page and the next to write down some signs you can see that your manifestation will soon be here.

_____

_____

_____

_____

_____

_____

_____

_____

_____

_____

_____

_____

_____

_____

_____

_____

Positive Signs

Look around you. Everywhere, you'll see signs that your dreams are about to arrive. Your attention to your positive energy has begun to pay off. The signs are there if you take the time to observe. Use the space below to record your observations.

What signs do you see that your dream is about to arrive?

DAILY 369 METHOD

MORNING: Write your manifestation statement
3 times when you first wake up.

1. _____
2. _____
3. _____

MIDDAY: (Daily Gratitude) Write 6 things
you are grateful to have in your life.

1. _____
2. _____
3. _____
4. _____
5. _____
6. _____

NIGHT: Before you go to bed, write out
your manifestation statement 9 times.

1. _____
2. _____
3. _____
4. _____
5. _____
6. _____
7. _____
8. _____
9. _____

DAILY **369** METHOD

MORNING: Write your manifestation statement
3 times when you first wake up.

1. _____
2. _____
3. _____

MIDDAY: (Daily Gratitude) Write 6 things
you are grateful to have in your life.

1. _____
2. _____
3. _____
4. _____
5. _____
6. _____

NIGHT: Before you go to bed, write out
your manifestation statement 9 times.

1. _____
2. _____
3. _____
4. _____
5. _____
6. _____
7. _____
8. _____
9. _____

DAILY 369 METHOD

MORNING: Write your manifestation statement
3 times when you first wake up.

1. _____
2. _____
3. _____

MIDDAY: (Daily Gratitude) Write 6 things
you are grateful to have in your life.

1. _____
2. _____
3. _____
4. _____
5. _____
6. _____

NIGHT: Before you go to bed, write out
your manifestation statement 9 times.

1. _____
2. _____
3. _____
4. _____
5. _____
6. _____
7. _____
8. _____
9. _____

DAILY 369 METHOD

MORNING: Write your manifestation statement
3 times when you first wake up.

1. _____
2. _____
3. _____

MIDDAY: (Daily Gratitude) Write 6 things
you are grateful to have in your life.

1. _____
2. _____
3. _____
4. _____
5. _____
6. _____

NIGHT: Before you go to bed, write out
your manifestation statement 9 times.

1. _____
2. _____
3. _____
4. _____
5. _____
6. _____
7. _____
8. _____
9. _____

DAILY 369 METHOD

MORNING: Write your manifestation statement
3 times when you first wake up.

1. _____
2. _____
3. _____

MIDDAY: (Daily Gratitude) Write 6 things
you are grateful to have in your life.

1. _____
2. _____
3. _____
4. _____
5. _____
6. _____

NIGHT: Before you go to bed, write out
your manifestation statement 9 times.

1. _____
2. _____
3. _____
4. _____
5. _____
6. _____
7. _____
8. _____
9. _____

DAILY 369 METHOD

MORNING: Write your manifestation statement
3 times when you first wake up.

1. _____
2. _____
3. _____

MIDDAY: (Daily Gratitude) Write 6 things
you are grateful to have in your life.

1. _____
2. _____
3. _____
4. _____
5. _____
6. _____

NIGHT: Before you go to bed, write out
your manifestation statement 9 times.

1. _____
2. _____
3. _____
4. _____
5. _____
6. _____
7. _____
8. _____
9. _____

DAILY **369** METHOD

MORNING: Write your manifestation statement
3 times when you first wake up.

1. _____
2. _____
3. _____

MIDDAY: (Daily Gratitude) Write 6 things
you are grateful to have in your life.

1. _____
2. _____
3. _____
4. _____
5. _____
6. _____

NIGHT: Before you go to bed, write out
your manifestation statement 9 times.

1. _____
2. _____
3. _____
4. _____
5. _____
6. _____
7. _____
8. _____
9. _____

DAILY 369 METHOD

MORNING: Write your manifestation statement
3 times when you first wake up.

1. _____
2. _____
3. _____

MIDDAY: (Daily Gratitude) Write 6 things
you are grateful to have in your life.

1. _____
2. _____
3. _____
4. _____
5. _____
6. _____

NIGHT: Before you go to bed, write out
your manifestation statement 9 times.

1. _____
2. _____
3. _____
4. _____
5. _____
6. _____
7. _____
8. _____
9. _____

DAILY 369 METHOD

MORNING: Write your manifestation statement
3 times when you first wake up.

1. _____
2. _____
3. _____

MIDDAY: (Daily Gratitude) Write 6 things
you are grateful to have in your life.

1. _____
2. _____
3. _____
4. _____
5. _____
6. _____

NIGHT: Before you go to bed, write out
your manifestation statement 9 times.

1. _____
2. _____
3. _____
4. _____
5. _____
6. _____
7. _____
8. _____
9. _____

Celebrate Yourself

You have come so far since you started this journey. Celebrate yourself! Use this space to reflect on what you are proud of and how you feel now that you have manifested your dreams.

Use this space to describe how you will reward yourself for your success! Use sensory details to manifest the positive energy.

Use this space to write the story of your success. Describe where you were when you started, the obstacles you overcame, and your final success. Write about yourself in third person so that you can recognize your success as others would.